"ARE
WE THERE
YET?"

TRAVEL GAMES FOR KIDS

This Book of Travel Games Belongs to

_____

"ARE WE THERE YET?"

TRAVEL GAMES FOR KIDS

Written and Illustrated by **RICHARD SALTER**

Prince Paperbacks
New York

*This book is dedicated
to Paris,
the only destination of
my heart.*

A Prince Paperback book. Published by Crown Publishers, Inc.,
201 East 50th Street, New York, New York 10022. Member of the Crown Publishing Group.

PRINCE PAPERBACKS and colophon are trademarks of Crown Publishers, Inc.

Manufactured in the United States of America

Library of Congress Cataloging-in-Publication Data
Salter, Richard, 1942–
    "Are we there yet?" travel games for kids / Richard Salter. – 1st ed.
        p.   cm.
    1. Games for travelers—Juvenile literature.   I. Title.
GV1206.S25   1991
794—dc20   90–22189
                                                                                      CIP
                                                                                      AC

ISBN 0–517–58304–6 (pbk.)

10   9   8   7   6   5

Contents

"ARE WE THERE YET?"

TRAVEL GAMES FOR KIDS

TAKE-OFF GAMES

Cargo

That's *right!* It's Bingo on the *road* and its name is *CARGO!*

How Many Can Play? Two or three works best when using one playing square, but any number can play if you make up more squares (they are easy to draw).

Best Playing Conditions: Any time, anywhere. Good to play when someone is sleeping.

Time Needed: 20 to 45 minutes.

Supplies: Pencil(s), playing square(s), and eyes like a hawk.

What's It All About?

To find the objects named in the boxes of the playing squares by looking outside your car.

How to Play

1. All players take time to look at the playing square so they know what objects to look for.
2. When all players are ready, everyone begins to look for the objects at the same time.
3. When a player spots one of the objects, he calls it out, circles it, and writes his initials inside its box at the bottom. (A different color pencil may be used for each player rather than writing in his initials if so desired.)

And the Winner Is...

The first player to spell C-A-R-G-O by finding all 5 objects across, down, or diagonally, as illustrated by the circles on the playing square.

CAUTION

An object can be used only by the player who spots it *first.* Other players must find other examples of the object.

C	A	R	G	O
driver not wearing seatbelt	school bus	cemetery	ski rack on car	20 MPH sign
truck carrying new cars	whitewall tires	car with dark tinted windows	car with no front plate	motorcycle
Open 24 Hours sign	blue and white hospital sign	fire hydrant	yellow Volkswagen	car with missing hubcap
car with convertible top	mobil home being towed	No Radio sign	bicycle	army vehicle
Jeep	an "Official" license plate	animal in car	car with luggage rack	out-of-state plate

Remember, when players get tired of looking for these objects you can draw a new square and fill in the boxes with new items you see on the road.

3

The Mating Sign Game

Here's a game where your signs of success are matched by your signs on the road.

How Many Can Play? Any number.

Best Playing Conditions: In and around town where there are the most signs along the road.

Time Needed: 30 minutes to an hour.

Supplies: 20 reusable paper or cardboard squares and a flat surface like the back seat, armrest, or a small suitcase.

To Get Ready

1. Cut or fold and tear 20 squares of equal size from a sheet of paper. (To make more permanent playing squares, cut them from a piece of cardboard and store them in a plastic sandwich bag.)
2. Neatly print the names of the signs listed here on *one* side of the square, one sign on each square, for a total of 20.

STOP	NO TURNS
DEAD END	MERGE
ONE WAY	EXIT
YIELD	EXIT ONLY
HOSPITAL	HILL
TELEPHONE	DO NOT ENTER
FALLEN ROCK ZONE	
UNLAWFUL TO LITTER	
SPEED ZONE AHEAD	
PASSENGER CARS ONLY	
SPEED CHECKED BY RADAR	
KEEP RIGHT (EXCEPT TO PASS)	
NO TURN ON RED	
SLIPPERY WHEN WET	

3. One player arranges the squares so they are all face down (so the printed sides can't be seen).
4. Next, shuffle the squares.
5. Then players choose a flat surface and one player deals all the squares out, face down in equal rows.

CAUTION

Players are not allowed to look at the printed side of the squares.

How to Play

1. Players go one at a time and in order.
2. Each player chooses a sign from the road, says its name out loud, and then, by turning just one square over (face up), tries to find the one with her sign on it.
3. If the right square is turned over (this is called a "match"), the

player keeps the square and goes again. But if a wrong square is turned over, the player shows the square to all the players, and then returns it to the same spot it was in before it was picked up. Now the next player goes.

And the Winner Is . . .

The player who has the most squares after they are all picked up, or when an agreed-upon time limit is reached.

(1.) Players should familiarize themselves with the sign list before beginning. (2.) You can make up a different sign list for your local area, or use multiples of the same sign if you want to make the game easier. (Example: three Stop signs, three One Way, three Yield, three Exit, etc.)

Gold-Plated States

There's gold in them plates from the states, but how much it's worth is one player's word against another's!

How Many Can Play? A minimum of two, but up to as many as you can fit in the car.
Best Playing Conditions: Long highway trips are best.
Time Needed: 1 to 3 hours.
Supplies: Pencil and paper for each player.

How to Play

1. First, each player chooses her own six- or seven-digit license plate from the cars she sees and writes the numbers and letters down on paper. (All players must use the same number of digits.)
2. Then, using the Number Conversion Chart, each player converts the numbers on her plate into *letters*.
3. Next, in a 15-minute play period, all players form as many words as they can with their letters, and write them down on paper. Words can be of any length, up to a limit of 6 or 7 letters, depending on the number of digits in the plates. Letters can be used more than once in *different* words, but not in the same word.

Example: With letters ATBEHH, B<u>EA</u>T and H<u>EA</u>T are okay but B<u>EE</u>T is not.

4. When time is up, all players add up the points for each word they've formed using the Letter Value Chart.
5. Finally, all players go on the 5-minute DOUBLE and TRIPLE CARAT Word Search by looking for their *words* outside the car (on signs, stores, billboards, etc.) or the *objects described* by any of the words they have formed. The DOUBLE CARAT WORD SCORE is awarded to each player who finds a *word* she has formed *written* outside the car. If one is found, the original value of the word is *doubled*. The TRIPLE CARAT WORD SCORE is awarded to each player who finds outside the car the *object described* by a word she has formed. If one of these is found, the original value of the word is *tripled*.

NOTE: During the 15-minute play period, players who wish to "dump" their plates for new ones may do so *once*, but their points can come from only *one* plate.

BONUS SCORE: Any player who forms a word using all the letters on her plate is awarded a bonus of 30 points.

And the Winner Is . . .

The player who's accumulated the most points after all rounds have been played.

Gold-Plated States
Sample Game

The Pohl family decides to play the game. Since Mrs. Pohl is driving, she agrees to be timekeeper for Mr. Pohl and their two boys, Greg and Evan. Mr. Pohl, Greg, and Evan each have pencil and paper. Each player takes a few minutes to find his own six-digit

plate. Then, using the Number Conversion Chart, they change their numbers into letters:

Mr. Pohl
MLF 599 = MLFEII

Greg
ATB 588 = ATBEHH

Evan
BPU 831 = BPUHCA

When all players are ready, Mrs. Pohl checks the clock and announces the start of the 15-minute play period. When time is up, she says "Stop," and each player adds up the points he has for the words he's formed.

Mr. Pohl
MLFEII

MILE = $3 + 1 + 2 + 1 = 7$
FILE = $4 + 1 + 2 + 1 = 8$
ELF = $\quad 1 + 2 + 4 = 7$
LIE = $\quad 2 + 1 + 1 = \underline{4}$
$\qquad\qquad\qquad\qquad 26$

Greg
ATBEHH

BAT = $\quad 2 + 1 + 2 = 5$
TAB = $\quad 2 + 1 + 2 = 5$
BEAT = $2 + 1 + 1 + 2 = 6$
HAT = $\quad 3 + 1 + 2 = 6$
HEAT = $3 + 1 + 1 + 2 = 7$
BET = $\quad 2 + 1 + 2 = \underline{5}$
$\qquad\qquad\qquad\qquad 34$

Evan
BPUHCA

CAP = $\qquad 3 + 1 + 3 = 7$
CUP = $\qquad 3 + 1 + 3 = 7$
HUBCAP = $3 + 1 + 2 + 3 + 1 + 3 = 13$
CAB = $\qquad 3 + 1 + 2 = \underline{6}$
$\qquad\qquad\qquad\qquad 33$

After all the totals are in, Mrs. Pohl announces the start of the 5-minute DOUBLE and TRIPLE CARAT Word Search. When the 5 minutes are up, all players tally their scores:

Mr. Pohl finds his word *mile* on a road sign and adds another 7 to his score (thereby doubling the original value of this word) for the DOUBLE CARAT and a total of 33 points $(26 + 7 = 33)$.

Greg finds his word *heat* on a billboard and adds another 7 points to his score (thereby doubling the original value of this word) for the DOUBLE CARAT; but then he also sees a driver in another car *wearing* a *hat* and adds 12 more points (12 added to the original value of *hat* [6] triples its value) for the TRIPLE CARAT, for a grand total of 53 points $(34 + 7 + 12)$.

Evan is doing very well. Although he finds none of his words *written* outside the car, he sees an object he's described, *hubcap*, on *every* car and can therefore add 26 points (26 added to the original value of *hubcap* [13] triples its value) to his score for the TRIPLE CARAT. Since he has used all six letters in *hubcap*, he gets 30 bonus points for a grand total of 89 $(33 + 26 + 30)$.

After the first round, Evan is in the lead with 89 points. The second round can now begin with all players choosing new plates.

Coast: The Mystery Word Game

Watch out, all you bluffers, fakers, and deceivers, there may be a spelling bee champ in the car.

How Many Can Play? Any number.

Best Playing Conditions: When things get really boring and no other games will do.

Time Needed: 20 to 40 minutes.

Supplies: Word lovers who can spell and bluff with the best of them, pencil and paper as needed, and maybe a pocket dictionary.

How to Get Coasting

1. Playing by the rules of Ghost, player #1 begins the game by saying the first letter of a mystery word he has in mind.
2. Next, going one at a time and in order, each player must add a letter to the one that came before *and have a word in mind* as the game continues in round-robin fashion.
3. Bluffing is allowed, but challenges must be made *before* another letter is added to the one in question.
4. Players drop out of the game if they cannot add to the word, if a word is formed with the letter they add, or if they cannot successfully defend a challenge from another player.

And the Winner Is...

The one player who remains after all the others have been eliminated.

Carbon Copy

Here's a game just like MATING SIGNS except it's played with car makes instead of road signs.

How Many Can Play? Any number.

Best Playing Conditions: Town, city, or highway travel where you will see plenty of cars.

Time Needed: 30 minutes to 1 hour.

Supplies: 25 reusable paper or cardboard playing cards; a flat surface like the back seat or armrest... and a good memory.

Players are not allowed to look at the printed side of the cards!

CAUTION

To Get Ready

1. Cut or fold and tear 25 squares of equal size from a sheet of paper or cardboard. (Remember, you can store them in a plastic sandwich bag!)
2. Then, neatly print the names of the cars listed on one side of the cards, one car on each card, for a total of 25.

AUDI	HONDA	PONTIAC
BMW	HYUNDAI	PORSCHE
BUICK	ISUZU	SAAB
CADILLAC	LINCOLN	SUBARU
CHEVROLET	MAZDA	TOYOTA
CHRYSLER	MERCEDES	VOLKSWAGEN
NISSAN	OLDSMOBILE	VOLVO
DODGE	PEUGEOT	
FORD	PLYMOUTH	

3. Arrange all the cards face down so the printed side cannot be seen.
4. Next, one player shuffles the cards.
5. Then, players choose a flat surface and one player deals all the cards out face down in equal rows.

How to Play

1. Players go one at a time and in order.
2. Alanna begins by choosing a car from the road, says its name out loud, and then, by turning just one card over (face up), tries to find the card with her car's name on it.
3. If the right card is chosen (this is called a "match"), she keeps the card and goes again. But if a wrong card is chosen, the player shows the card to all of the other players, and then returns it to the same spot it was in before it was picked up. Now Trevor may go.

And the Winner Is...

The player who has the most cards after they are all picked up.

20 *Carstions*

Here's a great way to have 30 minutes of fun without even looking outside the car. It's 20 Questions modified for the road.

How Many Can Play? Any number.
Best Playing Conditions: Whenever you like, regardless of traffic conditions.
Time Needed: 20 to 40 minutes.
Supplies: Pencil and paper (if you want to keep score).

How to Play

1. Player #1 thinks of an object inside the car. Small things are best ... like that little piece of hamburger roll down on the carpet.
2. Other players are allowed 20 *car*stions (in total, not 20 each) to guess what the object is.
3. Questions asked must be answerable by "yes" or "no" responses only.
4. If the players have not found the object after the twentieth *car*stion, player #1 is the winner of the round and reveals the object. The game continues with player #2 finding a new object for the other players to try to identify.

First try to determine which area of the car the object is in (front seat, back seat, left or right of center dashboard, etc.) Don't waste *carstions* by guessing wildly.

And the Winner Is...

The player who has won the most rounds.

11

The "Driving Me Crazy" Decarthlon

Like a real decathlon, all players advance through a series of ten events in the order that they appear.

How Many Can Play? Any number.
Best Playing Conditions: Long highway travel is best.
Time Needed: 1 to 2 hours.
Supplies: Pencil, paper, patience, and determination.

How to Play

1. All players begin at the same time and look for their *own* items in each event.
2. While they are going through their events, players watch out for "jumps" and "bumps" as listed below. A "jump" gives a player the power to skip over any event of his choice *except* #10. A "bump" gives a player the power to move any other player back to repeat the event just completed. Each player is allowed to use one jump and one bump during the de*car*thlon, and they can be saved for use at any time.
3. All findings must be confirmed by at least one other player or someone not in the de*car*thlon.
4. Once a player reaches event #10 he cannot be bumped back to #9.

The Events

1. Find 5 vehicles in any of the following colors: red, gray, yellow, green, blue, white, or black.
2. Make a female driver of another car wave at you, or in another car find a woman wearing a hat.
3. Choose one of the following two assignments (**A** or **B**). **A)** Find a clock of any kind outside the car, say the time out loud (Example: "Three forty-two"), and then find these three numbers (or four, as the case may be) 3, 4, 2 on one license plate. Found numbers do not have to be in sequence, but if they are, the player may skip the #4 event and go on to #5. **B)** Find the letters A through F, in order, taking one letter from each of six separate license plates.
4. Find a person sitting backwards (opposite direction of travel) in a vehicle, a male passenger smok-

JUMPS

A moving fire truck

An ambulance, EMS truck, or MD plate

A US Mail truck

BUMPS

A temporary license plate inside rear window of car

A bike rack on the rear end of a car with at least two bikes mounted

A cemetery

Example: PLM 754 =

P = Phone
L = Money
M = Money
7 = Seven = Seven, Stamp, etc.
5 = Five = First, Fishy, etc.
4 = Four = Funny, Favor, etc.

ing in another car, or an "Official" license plate.

5. Find an out-of-state license plate, write the numbers and letters down on paper, and make up a five-letter word for each letter and number on the plate. For numbers, convert each numeral into its word name (7 = Seven) and then use the first letter of the word to start a five-letter word.

6. Find a word on a sign with at least four letters in it and make it into a sentence. (Example: Stop = She Tasted Olivia's Pizza.) Those players who pick signs with six letters or more and make complete sentences of them can jump event #7 and go on to #8. (Example: Dead End = David Esterley and Dolly Eubanks never drive.)

7. Find a plane in the sky, or a college decal on a rear window, or a station wagon.

8. Find a car with something hanging from its rearview mirror, a car with whitewall tires, or a car with an animal in it.

9. Find a car with a "Get It Together" seatbelt decal on its side window, a wheel with no hubcap on it, or, a car with at least five people in it.

10. Find a car with something on top of it (luggage, skis, bikes, mattress, etc.), say out loud, "I'm about to win the decarthlon," and then get anyone outside your car to wave at you.

And the Winner Is...

The first player to advance through all ten events. However, if players cannot get through all ten events, a time limit can be used. Then the winner would be the player who gets closest to the last event.

Target Practice

How Many Can Play? Any number. You can play in teams, too!

Best Playing Conditions: City, town, or highway travel, or wherever you will see lots of numbers.

Time Needed: It's up to you.

Supplies: Pencil and paper for each player, and target-shooters with a mathematical aim.

How to Play

1. All players decide on any one target number they will all try to reach by adding other numbers together. Example: target number 27 ($3 + 6 + 9 + 4 + 5 = 27$)

2. Players can go all at once, or, if this gets too exciting, 30-second time limits can be used, with players going one at a time.

3. Using any variety of road signs (speed limits, route numbers, store and house numbers, exits, etc.) and/or license plates, players pick their own numbers, call them out as they see them, and record them on paper.

4. As numbers are added, players keep a running total to remember how close they are getting to the target.

5. All players must land *exactly* on the target number with the last number they choose. If the target number is **27**, and Carol has a 9, a 6, and an 8, she must find a 4 to take the game in one shot.

And the Winner Is . . .

The first player to land exactly on the target number.

Advanced Target Practice

For sharpshooters only!

How to Play

1. All players decide on a target number, just as in TARGET PRACTICE. But then, each player *predicts* how many shots it will take him to hit the target number exactly on the nose. Example: "I can hit that target number 27 in five shots."
2. In this more difficult variety of the game, players should go one at a time, for a length of time they agree on.
3. All other rules remain the same.

And the Winner Is...

That player who first hits the target number on the *last* of his predicted number of shots.

NOTE FOR SUPER-SHARPSHOOTERS: Try predicting the number of shots you will take *and* a time limit! Example: "I can hit that target number in six shots, in less than 3 minutes."

Getting to the Doctor

In this game, a trip to the doctor can be nothing but fun... unless you hit a lot of "bumps" along the way.

How Many Can Play? Any number.

Best Playing Conditions: Highway or town driving when traffic is medium to heavy.

Time Needed: 20 to 45 minutes.

Supplies: Pencil, paper, and a good eye for numbers.

Players can make up their own "bump" lists to suit the area they are traveling through.

How It Works

Each of you is going to be looking for numbers 1 through 9 in consecutive order $(1,2,3,4\ldots)$. After reaching 9, each player must find a hospital, a hospital sign, a sign for a doctor's office, or an MD license plate in order to win the game. But... what if the road gets "bumpy"?

How to Play with the "Bumps"

1. Using numbers found on license plates, storefronts, houses, or road signs (speed limits, exits, route numbers, bridge clearance heights, billboards, mile markers, etc.), each player must find her own numbers 1 through 9 *in order,* and call them out as she sees them.

2. But... during the game, if a player spots any of the things on the "Bump" List, above right, she can bump any other player down to a lower number according to the list.

"BUMP" LIST	
Stop sign:	back one number
Flashing red traffic light:	back two numbers
Do Not Enter sign:	back three numbers
Tow truck; or Car being towed; or Car with its hood up:	back to #1

Doctor's Notes

1. Players who reach 9 cannot be bumped.
2. Players cannot be bumped until they reach 4.
3. No one can be bumped below 1.
4. Any player who spots an ambulance with its siren on and lights flashing is an automatic winner.

And the Winner Is...

The first player to "get to the doctor" after reaching 9.

16

The Odometer Game

Here's a fun way for all of you prognosticators to show your stuff.

How Many Can Play? Any number, plus one non-player to keep time and score.

Best Playing Conditions: Highway travel is best, regardless of traffic conditions.

Time Needed: 5 to 10 minutes.

Supplies: Trip odometer, pencil and paper for each player, and a good sense of time.

How to Play

1. Each player picks a number between 10 and 40, announces it to the other players, and writes it down on paper.
2. Driver starts the game by resetting the trip odometer (by the speedometer dial) and saying "Go."
3. As time goes by, each player calls out when he thinks his number has come up on the odometer dial.
4. When the nonplaying scorekeeper hears the call, he makes note of the *actual* number on the dial, and after all players have called, calculates the difference between the numbers guessed in Step 3 and the actual numbers on the dial.
5. Players can go in rounds until a time limit or mileage point is reached.

And the Winner Is...

The player with the *fewest* points when all the rounds are over.

The *Carbo*hydrate Game

How Many Can Play? Any number.
Best Playing Conditions: Highway or city travel where stores, factories, billboards, and signs are seen.
Time Needed: 1 hour or more.
Supplies: Pencil and paper for each player, and a sweet eye-tooth!

What's It All About?

Gaining and losing *car*lories, of course!

How to Put It On

1. Using the *Car*bo Point Chart opposite, all players search for "sweet things" and try to gain *car*lories to win the game.
2. All players go at once, point out and announce their findings, and then record their points on paper.

How to Take It Off

During the game, if any player spots an object on the Hydrate Chart, she may reduce the score of any player by its corresponding *car*lorie loss.

NOTE: Players cannot lose *car*lories until they have reached a total of 6, and cannot be reduced below 5.

And the Winner Is . . .

The first player to gain 15 *car*lories (or whatever total players decide on).

CARBO POINT CHART

5 carlorie gain: A factory or plant for candy, baked goods, ice cream, soda, or beer; an ice cream store or parlor; anyone eating ice cream, cake, or candy outside the car in pictures or in reality.

3 carlorie gain: A candy, pastry, bakery, or liquor store; a soda, bakery, or ice cream truck or van; any sign or billboard advertising any of the above.

1 carlorie gain: Anyone outside the car drinking any beverage through a straw; any soda machine; any soda or beer can (or bottle) outside the car; one license plate with any of the following numbers (in order) or letters (in order or scrambled) on it: 16, 18, 20, FAT, BIG, SODA, CAL, DDS, LG, XXL, XL, EE, EEE.

HYDRATE CHART

1 carlorie loss: A fire hydrant

2 carlorie loss: A fire house or parked fire truck or car

3 carlorie loss: A fire alarm box, moving fire truck, or someone jogging

4 carlorie loss: A fire truck with lights and siren on, or two people jogging together

5 carlorie loss: A lake, river, or stream, or an exercise center

7 carlorie loss: A fire being fought

The "I'm Hungry" Game

Okay, all you starving travelers, here's your chance to *whine* and dine, but only in your mind.

How Many Can Play? Any number.
Best Playing Conditions: When your driver doesn't want to stop for something to eat.
Time Needed: 15 to 30 minutes.
Supplies: Good memories, and menus just as big as your stomach!

How to Set the Table

1. All diners are going to be thinking of food orders that begin with each consecutive letter of the alphabet (A, B, C, etc.). Example: apple juice, American cheese, artichoke; banana bread, bacon cheeseburger, blueberry pancakes
2. Each diner must repeat all of the orders that preceded his own, and then add a new one that begins with the next letter of the alphabet.

How to Be Excused from the Table

Diners who cannot remember previous food orders, think of new items to add, or bear to talk about food anymore are excused from the table!

Diners can set their own time limits for each turn.

And the Winner Is ...

The sole surviving diner whose memory is just as big as his stomach.

Fast-Food Takeover

This game should be played only after everyone has eaten!

How Many Can Play? Any number.
Best Playing Conditions: During long or very boring highway trips.
Time Needed: 45 to 90 minutes.
Supplies: Pencil and paper for each player, and an appetite for *corporate* takeovers.

How to Play

1. All players decide on a time limit for the game. (45 minutes, 1 hour, etc.)
2. Next, each player selects a fast-food restaurant that she will be the owner of for the rest of the game.

SAMPLE RESTAURANTS

Arby's	Howard Johnson's
Bob's Big Boy	Roy Rogers
Burger King	7-Eleven
Carvel	McDonald's
Domino's Pizza	Pizza Hut
Friendly's	Wendy's

---

3. All restauranteurs begin to look for their restaurant on or off the road, and their restaurant's name on billboards, exit markers, and Food/Fuel signs, and listen for their restaurant's name on the radio.
4. All findings are worth 1 point.

Owners call them out as they see them, and record them on paper.

How to Get Stomachaches

After all owners have 2 points or more:

- If Beth spots Chuck's restaurant before Chuck does, Beth gets 1 point and Chuck loses 1 point.
- If Beth makes Chuck's score go down to 0, Beth *takes over* Chuck's restaurant and uses it to get more points along with her own.
- The only way for Chuck to get his restaurant back is to get a point from it before Beth does. But, while Chuck doesn't have his restaurant, he can still get points by spotting other owners' restaurants before they do.

And the Winner Is...

The owner who has the most points when the game time is over.

Shooting for the Moon

Here's a game that players should begin around dusk, when drivers start to put their headlights on. It's also a good game for passengers who can't fall asleep.

How Many Can Play? Any number.
Best Playing Conditions: After the sun goes down; during highway travel, medium to heavy traffic.
Time Needed: 30 minutes to 1 hour.
Supplies: Pencil and paper for each player.

What's It All About?

To find your way up to the top of the Night Light List before anyone else does.

How to Play

1. All players write the letters A through M on their paper, in a vertical row starting at the bottom of the page.
2. All at the same time, players start at the *bottom* of the list and look for the items in the order that they appear. As they find them, they make a check (√) mark beside the letter.
3. While the game is in progress, any player who finds a car with only one headlight on can move any other player back down the list to find the previously found item again.

How to Get and Make a Pass

Each player is allowed a maximum of three passes, which can be used to skip a hard-to-find item and move up to the next one. Players can get passes only by finding license plates with double zeros on them (00) or cars with three people sitting in the front seat. Passes can be saved and used at any time during the game, but cannot be used for the last item, M.

And the Winner Is . . .

The player who gets to the top of the Night Light List first.

NIGHT LIGHT LIST

END

M _____ a star in the sky (if it's too cloudy, skip this and find the moon instead)

L _____ a car with interior dome light on

K _____ an airplane in the sky

J _____ a car with broken taillight (white light showing through broken cover)

I _____ a car with headlights off in the dark

H _____ an Open 24 Hours sign

G _____ a hotel or motel sign lit up

F _____ a neon Vacancy or No Vacancy sign lit up

E _____ a revolving gas station sign lit up

D _____ a nonrevolving gas station sign lit up

C _____ a car with only its parking lights on

B _____ a street or highway light turned on

A _____ a car with its headlights on

START

The Electric Night Light

What's It All About?

Finding the right lights in the night.

How to Play

1. Players begin together. Each player must find the colors red, orange (amber), yellow, green, blue, and white in this order, *only* from electric light sources that are turned on.
2. As players find their lights, they call them out and keep track of their own scores.
3. In the course of the game, each player is entitled to one "jump," which can be used to skip one color and go on to the next. A jump is awarded to the player who first sees a car with only one headlight on.
4. All citings must be confirmed by at least one other player or someone not playing the game.

NOTE: If a player wants to use a car's taillights for the color red, they must be on a car with at least 2 red lights on either side.

And the Winner Is . . .

The first player to find the white night light.

Stars are not electric light sources!

24

COLOR GAMES

The Car Color Games (I, II, and III)

Here are three easy-to-play games in which players look for cars of a specific color.

How Many Can Play? Any number.
Best Playing Conditions: Medium to heavy town or highway traffic.
Time Needed: 15 to 30 minutes.
Supplies: Pencil and paper for each player, and sharp eyes for color.

I. For Junior Players:

How to Play

1. Players decide on a time limit.
2. Next they decide if they will look for the target colors in the order listed below, or in random order.
3. When players are ready, the timekeeper says "Go," and all players try to find one car in each of the following colors: red, orange, yellow, green, blue, brown (or beige), white, and black.

And the Winner Is...

The first player to find all the colors, or the most colors within the time limit of the game.

II. For Intermediate Players:

How to Play

1. Players decide on a winning point total (10, 15, 20, etc.).
2. Next, each player chooses a color (or colors) that *only he or she* will look for. Players must use *different* colors.
3. When everyone's ready, all players go at the same time, call out their findings, and keep a running total of their score on paper.

Scoring Rules

All cars of *one* color are worth 1 point. Two-tone cars of the same color are worth 2 points. (Example: dark green on top and light green on the bottom.)

25

Two-tone cars of different colors are worth ½ point. (Example: player picks red. The car observed is white on top and red on the bottom.)

And the Winner Is...

The first player to reach or pass the winning point total.

III. For Advanced Players:

How to Play

In this game, each player chooses not only the color of the cars he will look for but also the makes and models of cars in specific color.

1. Players decide on a winning point total.
2. Each player chooses two colors that he will be looking for on *any* car.
3. Next, each player writes down five predictions of car *makes* of a certain color. (Examples: white Cadillac, black Porsche, gray Ford, etc.)
4. Then, each player writes down five predictions of car makes *and* models of a certain color. (Examples: yellow Honda Accord, white Volkswagen Fox, black Ford Thunderbird, etc.)
5. When all players are ready, they begin to look for their predictions, call them out when they spot them, and record their scores.

Scoring Rules

1 point for finding a car in one of the chosen colors.
2 points for finding the color and make.
3 points for finding color, make, and model.

And the Winner Is...

The player who reaches the agreed-upon winning point total first.

The Car Towing Game

If you've ever been with Mom or Dad when the car's been towed away, you know how bad it feels. If you haven't, this game may give you some idea of how it *does* feel! Why? Because you are going to be parking and towing cars.

How Many Can Play? Two.
Best Playing Conditions: In town or the city where traffic is medium to heavy.
Time Needed: 20 to 30 minutes.
Supplies: Pencil and paper for each player and a cool head!

What's It All About?

Players are looking for cars of different colors, and "parking" them on their side of the Parking Lot.

How to Play

1. First, both players familiarize themselves with the colors of the cars they will be looking for, as listed in the Parking Lot.
2. Both players start looking at the same time for one car of each color.
3. Each player finds his own car. Once a car is found it cannot be used by the other player, who must look for another car of the same color.
4. When cars are found, players call out the color (Example: "Dark blue, over there," or "Red Honda, behind the bus") and write it down on their paper.

PARKING LOT

Player 1		Player 2
_____	Red	_____
_____	Maroon	_____
_____	Dark Blue	_____
_____	Green	_____
_____	Brown/Tan	_____
_____	White	_____
_____	Black	_____
_____	Gray	_____
_____	Light Blue	_____
_____	Orange	_____
_____	Yellow	_____

How You Can Get into Trouble:

While you are playing, if your opponent sees any of the signs listed under No Parking Signs, he can tow any of your parked cars over to his side of the lot. Of course, if you see one, you can do the same to him.

27

No Parking Signs

No Parking Anytime
No Parking Between Signs
No Parking
No Standing Here to Corner
No Stopping or Standing
No Standing Anytime
Do Not Block Side Road

And the Winner Is...

The first player to get all of his cars parked on his side of the Parking Lot.

CAR MAKE GAMES

"Bug" Swatting

Here's a fun game for all Volkswagen (VW) "Beetle" or "Bug" lovers.

How Many Can Play? Any number.

Best Playing Conditions: Highway or city where traffic is medium to heavy; best for long highway trips.

Time Needed: 1 to 2 hours, depending on the winning point total set by players.

Supplies: Pencil and paper for each player, and a good eye for "Beetles."

What's It All About?

To spot and "swat" VW Beetles along the road until a winning game total is reached.

How to Start Swatting

1. Using the Point Distribution Chart at right, all players begin at the same time, announce their findings, and record their scores on paper.
2. Points are awarded only to the player who spots the car and says "swatbuggy" before anyone else can.

How to Get De-Bugged:

During the game, any player who sees a moving garbage truck and calls

POINT DISTRIBUTION CHART

"Bug" Color:

red, orange, or yellow	1 point
blue, green, or white	2 points
black	3 points
brown or tan	4 points
any other color	5 points
2 tone or more	6 points

Bonus "Bug" Points:

convertible with top up	1 point
convertible with top down	2 points
Bug with vanity plate (with numbers and letters)	3 points
Bug with vanity plate (with letters only)	4 points
Bug with vanity plate (with no numbers and referring to itself) Example: BUG OUT, BUGGED, BEETLE, etc.	5 points

it out first can take 2 points off any other player's score. De-bugging cannot be done until a player has 5 points, and a player's score cannot be reduced below 5 points.

Sample Play

Grady has 40 points. On a side street he sees a parked Beetle convertible with yellow paint, the top down, and a vanity plate reading "123 GO." He will get 1 point for yellow, 2 points for the top down, and 3 points for the vanity plate with numbers and letters, for a total of 6 more points. Michele now spots a garbage truck turning the corner, calls it out first, and decides to take 2 points off Grady's score since he is in the lead.

 Don't forget to say "swat-buggy"!

CAUTION

And the Winner Is . . .

The first "bugswatter" to reach the winning game total decided by the players.

And the Anytime, Automatic Winner Is . . .

The first player who sees a convertible Bug with whitewall tires on all four wheels.

Carnation

Here's a game to test your knowledge of cars, cities, and countries.

How Many Can Play? Any number.
Best Playing Conditions: Whenever you're ready; even if you're the only car on the road.
Time Needed: 10 to 20 minutes.
Supplies: Pencil, paper, and a timekeeper.

What's It All About?

To join together, end-to-end, the names of car makes and models with the names of cities or countries around the world.

How to Play

1. Players go in turns. Player #1 begins by naming a car make or model. Example: Toyot<u>a</u>.
2. Within 30 seconds, player #2 must give the name of a city or country that begins with A, the last letter of Toyot<u>a</u>. Example: Ann Arbo<u>r</u>.
3. Continuing in this manner, the next player has 30 seconds to name a *different* car make or model that begins with R, the final letter of Ann Arbo<u>r</u>. Example: Rolls Royc<u>e</u>.
4. No repeats are allowed. If a player cannot think of a car, country, or city, he is "out."

And the Winner Is . . .

Whoever is left after all other players are eliminated or the player who wins the most rounds.

The Foreign Affair

Here's a game for players who really know the names of cars and what they *look* like. (American cars and the "foreign affairs.")

How Many Can Play? Any number.
Best Playing Conditions: Highway travel with medium to heavy traffic.
Time Needed: 15 to 45 minutes.
Supplies: Pencil and paper.

How to Play

1. Player #1 picks a number greater than 10 and begins counting the cars traveling in the opposite direction until the car corresponding to his number appears. This car is her target car.

2. When she sees it, she must name the make or model of this car. If she cannot name it, she must begin counting, out loud, (1, 2, 3 . . .) every car that comes after her target car until she sees a foreign car ("foreign affair") that she can correctly name.

3. If a player correctly names her target car, her score for that round is zero, and the next player goes. If she cannot correctly name her target car, her score is the last number she calls out before identifying her foreign affair. (Players can decide how high this penalty number can go.)

4. Players continue in turns and record their scores as they get them. After an agreed-upon number of rounds, scores are added up.

And the Winner Is . . .

The player with the *lowest* score after all the rounds are played.

*Car*ismatic *Car*acters

Here's a good *car*acter-building game that's guaranteed to liven up the most boring trip to any place.

How Many Can Play? Any number.

Best Playing Conditions: Any time you need to burn some time.

Time Needed: 20 to 40 minutes.

Supplies: Pencil and paper for each player, timekeeper, and a memory for *car*ismatic *car*acters.

How to Play

1. First, using his or her own paper, each player writes down the names of five to ten (you decide the number) car makes in a vertical row on the left side of the page.
2. Players set a time limit for the game.
3. Then, when the timekeeper says "Go," each player hunts for famous people's initials that are hidden in the names of their cars.

Example: O L D S M O B I L E =

Steve Martin
Billy Idol
Diane Sawyer

NOTE: In this game, common letters shared by two names (like the s in the example) can be used more than once, and the same initials can be used as many times as a player likes.

4. One point is given for each correct *car*acter.

And the Winner Is...

The player with the most number of initials when the time limit is up.

The Wild *Card* Game

For those fidgety travelers in a gambling state of mind, here's a sure way to beat those monotonous highway odds.

How Many Can Play? Any number. **Best Playing Conditions:** City or highway trips when traffic is medium to heavy. **Time Needed:** 20 to 45 minutes. **Supplies:** Pencil and paper for each player, and a timekeeper.

To Get Started

1. Each player chooses a car and announces its name and color to the other players. (Example: maroon Honda, red Volvo, blue Chevrolet, etc.) This car will be your lucky "wild *car*d," which you will use to get bonus points in the game, so choose it carefully.

➡ It is best for players to pick a car and color that they think they will see on the road. (You may love black Jaguars, but you may never see one during your turn.)

2. Players now decide how many rounds they will play in the game. Since each player goes in a 60-second time period, if there are three players, one round will take about 4 to 5 minutes.

What's It All About?

To get as many points as you can in your turns from seeing target vehicles.

How to Play

1. Going one at a time, and in order, each player has 60 seconds to look for and choose only *one* of the target vehicles listed on the chart. Naturally, players will want to choose a target vehicle with as high a point value as they can find.

Target Vehicles	
Van	1 point
Truck	2 points
Jeep	3 points
Bus	4 points
Taxi	5 points
Motorcycle	6 points
Mobile Home	7 points

But if you see your wild *card* during your turn, you can take points for each and every target vehicle you see in your 60-second time limit! Each player records his score.

A Wild *Card* Example

During Vaughn's turn, he sees a van (worth 1 point). He can either take the van for 1 point and let Laurie go, or he can let the van go by and take a chance that he will see a higher-point-value target vehicle before his 60 seconds are up. If his luck runs out and he does not see a better target vehicle, his score for this turn is zero and Laurie's turn begins. However, if he sees his wild *card* at any time during his turn, he gets points for all of the target vehicles he can see before his turn is up.

And the Winner Is...

The player who has the most points at the end of the last round.

Ask your timekeeper to call out "15" when 15 seconds are up, "30" when 30 seconds are up, "45" when 45 seconds are up, and to count down (10, 9, 8, 7...) the last 10 seconds of each player's turn.

The Parking Lot Game

What's It All About?

This game is played like THE CAR TOWING GAME except with *makes* of cars instead of colors. Players will be looking for 12 different kinds of cars and trying to park them on their side of the lot.

How to Play

1. First, both players familiarize themselves with the target cars on the parking lot list.
2. Then, both players start looking for target cars at the same time.
3. A car found by one player cannot be used again by the other player, who must look for another one of the same make.
4. When a car is found, the player calls it out (Example: "Mercedes, over there in the gas station") and puts an X next to her space in the parking lot.

PARKING LOT

Jackie		John
————	Volkswagen	————
————	Audi	————
————	BMW	————
————	Cadillac	————
————	Nissan	————
————	Honda	————
————	Mercedes	
————	Ford	————
————	Chrysler	————
————	Porsche	————
————	Toyota	————
————	Saab	————

How to Lose Your Parked Cars

During the game, if Jackie sees any one of the No Parking Signs (listed below) she can take any car she needs from John's parked cars over to her side of the lot. And, of course, John can do the same thing to Jackie!

But if any target car is spotted either in a parking spot already or pulling into (not out of) one, the player calls, "Lock on that Mercedes over there!" and the car cannot be moved. Any player who finds a car under these circumstances (parked already or going into a parking spot) *cannot* have that car taken by her opponent. It is "locked" and hers for the rest of the game.

And the Winner Is . . .

The first player to get all of the target cars parked on her side of the lot.

No Parking Signs

No Parking Anytime
No Parking Between Signs
No Parking
No Standing Here to Corner
No Stopping or Standing
No Standing Anytime
Do Not Block Side Road

For those *car*sharks who need a bit more challenge in the game, try making up a new Parking Lot with makes *and* models in it. (Example: Volkswagen Fox, Mercedes 300SE, etc.)

Famous *Car*acters

Here's another game like CARISMATIC *CAR*ACTERS where players will be creating celebrities out of initials hidden in the names of cars.

What's It All About?

Players will be using all the famous people they can think of, so start digging up those names of your favorite singers, actors, actresses, athletes, TV personalities, rock stars, writers, musicians, painters, dancers, presidents, and anyone else that comes to your mind.

How to Play

1. Using separate pieces of paper, all players write the alphabet in a vertical column as shown in the example.
2. Next, one player thinks of car makes or models, and writes their names in vertically next to the letters in the alphabet column, creating a list of initials. The player announces the names as he enters them so all the players will have the same series of letters. (See the example again.)

It doesn't matter if the make or model letters don't end at the bottom of the alphabet, as long as the last letters are the beginning of another car.

3. After players decide on the length of the game, each one tries to make as many famous *car*acters as possible from the initials before the time limit is up.
4. One point is given for each correct *car*acter.

And the Winner Is...

The player with the most points when the time is up.

If you want the game to last longer, you can make up new car names and play in rounds.

AS *Arnold Schwartzenegger/Ally Sheedy*
BA
CA
DB *David Bowie*

EV *Eddie Van Halen*
FO
GL *George Lucas*
HV
IO

JF *Jodie Foster*
KO
LX

MJ *Michael Jordan/Michael Jackson*
NA
OG
PU
QA
RR *Richard Rodgers*

SM *Steve Martin*
TA
UZ
VD
WA

XL
YI
ZN

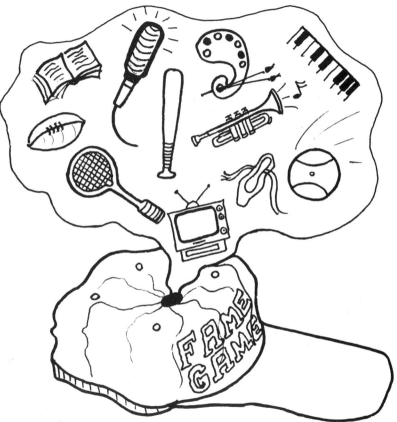

HUNTING GAMES

The Great Scarvenger Hunt (Three Levels of Difficulty)

Okay all you scavenger hunters, here's your chance to take your hunting skills on the road!

How Many Can Play? Any number.
Best Playing Conditions: Long highway trips are best, with medium to heavy traffic.
Time Needed: 45 to 90 minutes.
Supplies: Pencil and paper for each player, a timekeeper, and 360-degree, 20/20 vision.

How to Be a Scarvenger

In an agreed-upon time period, all hunters must find as many items as they can from the Fair Game Lists. They can hunt for the objects in any order they wish, and each item is worth 10 points.

How to Start the Hunt

1. All players familiarize themselves with the Fair Game List they will be using (there are three levels of difficulty).
2. Next, players decide how long their hunting period will last (20 minutes, 30 minutes, etc.) and if they want to play more than one period for the game.
3. Beginning together, players hunt for the items, call them out and show them to at least one other player when they are seen. Players write down the numbers of their items.
4. In all levels of THE GREAT SCARVENGER HUNT, an object can be used only by the hunter who finds it first. Other hunters must look for the item in another place.

And the Winner Is...

The hunter who's accumulated the most points at the end of the hunting period.

Make up your own Fair Game Lists so you can change or substitute when you like.

40

Level of Difficulty: Beginner

1. a 20 MPH sign
2. an arrow pointing to the right
3. a college decal in the rear window of a car
4. a church steeple
5. an MD license plate
6. initials of someone you know on a license plate
7. two whitewall tires on a car
8. a Stop sign
9. a car with at least three stickers on its rear bumper
10. the word *Turbo* on a car
11. a person wearing a set of headphones
12. a convertible car with the top up
13. a traffic light on green
14. a "Get It Together" seatbelt decal on a car window
15. a wheel with no hubcap on it

Level of Difficulty: Intermediate

1. a tow truck with a car in tow
2. a "piece" of graffiti
3. a ∅ prohibited sign
4. your initials on a license plate (in order)
5. a woman smoking in a car traveling in your direction
6. a tractor trailer with *16* wheels, not 18.
7. a car with real wire wheels (*not* imitation hubcaps)
8. a person moving to music in another car
9. an "Official" license plate
10. a "Don't Tailgate" bumper sticker
11. a temporary license plate in a rear window
12. a car with no license plate in front
13. a "No Radio" sign, or words to that effect
14. a DDS license plate
15. an AAA sticker anywhere on a car

(FAIR GAME LISTS continued)

Level of Difficulty: Expert

1. an "I ♡ my __" bumper sticker *not* showing a dog
2. a directional signal left on in the right-turn position
3. a horse carrier/trailer with a horse visible inside
4. driver of another car with arm around passenger
5. an empty billboard (saying "Put your ad here," etc.)
6. a ½ (fraction) on a road sign
7. an airline advertisement on a billboard or sign
8. a set of "Dealer" license plates
9. a spare wheel cover with animal illustration on it
10. a "For Sale" sign on a moving vehicle
11. a three-letter word on a vanity plate
12. a car with an object hanging from its rearview mirror
13. a movie marquee (single theater or mall multicinema)
14. a Falling Rock Zone sign
15. an Oversize Load or an Extra Wide Load sign on a truck

POINT DISTRIBUTION CHART

Zero to 30 points:	You need glasses; try another game; go back to sleep; forget it.
40 to 60 points:	Showing improvement; repeat basic training; study the signs.
70 to 90 points:	Okay; not bad; more practice; understudy for bird watcher; junior traffic controller.
100 to 120 points:	Great; retired spy; part-time work available as private detective.
130 to 150 points:	Sensational; fantastic; you're a roadhound; eye donor candidate; X-ray vision; hawkeye; Sherlock Mobilholmes.

The With or Without Game

Here's a simple way to have fun where players look for items on the With or Without lists.

> **How Many Can Play?** Two.
> **Best Playing Conditions:** In town or on the highway with medium to heavy traffic.
> **Time Needed:** 20 to 45 minutes.
> **Supplies:** Pencil and paper for each player.

Remember to make up your own lists when you get tired of these!

How to Play

1. Both players familiarize themselves with the suggested With and Without lists, and pick one they think they can win the game with. (*Highway Hint:* If players can't decide, flip a coin. Then switch lists on the next round.)
2. Next, players decide if they will find the items in the order they are listed, or in any order they want. They also decide if they want to impose a time limit or play until one player finds all ten items.
3. Both players begin looking at the same time, and each keeps her score.

And the Winner Is . . .

The first player to complete her list, or, if you're using a time limit, the one who finds the most items on the list within the time limit.

WITH

1. car with whitewall tires
2. car with "Get It Together" seatbelt decal
3. car with a 4 and a 6 on its plate
4. car with a luggage rack
5. car with real wire wheels
6. car with someone wearing glasses
7. car with driver's arm out window
8. car with at least 4 people in it
9. car with yellow "_____ On Board" sign
10. truck with trailer

WITHOUT

1. car without front plate
2. car without "Get It Together" seatbelt decal
3. car without 2, 4, 6, and 8 on its plate
4. car without rear window brake light
5. car without a hubcap
6. car with no one wearing glasses
7. car without 4 doors
8. car with no passengers
9. car with no men in it
10. truck without a trailer (tractor/cab only)

The Secret Place Race

Here is one of the quietest games in this book. While someone is napping, you can start mapping.

How Many Can Play? Two is best, but any number can play.
Best Playing Conditions: Anytime, anywhere, even when your little brother is sleeping.
Time Needed: 15 to 30 minutes.
Supplies: Pencil, paper, a timekeeper, and a regular road map.

To Get Ready

Fold a road map into a square or rectangle. This will be your playing surface.

To Get to the Secret Place:

1. Player #1 takes the map and finds a secret city, town, village, river, route number, lake, reservoir, or any hard-to-find location.
2. Next, she tells player #2 the name of the place she has chosen.
3. When the timekeeper says "Go," player #2 has 60 seconds to find the secret place.
4. If player #2 finds the secret place before time is up, the number of seconds he took is written down. If he does not find the secret place, his score is 60. No player can score more than 60 points per round.
5. Continue in this manner with player #2 choosing a secret place that the next player must find.

And the Winner Is . . .

The player with the lowest score after all rounds have been played.

True West's Animal Cemetery Game

During their trip to New Orleans, Tod and his friends are seeing many different kinds of animals outside the car. Tod suggests that they play the ANIMAL CEMETERY GAME.

How Many Can Play? Any number.

Best Playing Conditions: Long highway trips; cross-country traveling is ideal.

Time Needed: 1 to 2 hours or more.

Supplies: Pencil and paper for each player.

Here's How It Works

1. Going all at once, players look for the animals on the Species List, announce their findings, and record their points as they go along.
2. But whenever one of them first sees a cemetery, a golf course, or a swimming pool, that player *keeps* his points and all other players *lose* theirs.
3. Play continues in this way until a point total is reached or an agreed-upon time period is over.

SPECIES LIST

1 point: dogs and cats
2 points: cows, horses, and sheep
3 points: skunk, squirrels, pigs, groundhogs
4 points: deer, rabbit
5 points: people on horseback, horses or other animals working, and horses inside carriers

And the Winner Is...

The player with the highest point score at the end of play.

Trooper Scooper

*At last, it's **your** turn to chase after **them** for a change!*

How Many Can Play? Any number.

Best Playing Conditions: City or downtown driving when traffic is medium to heavy.

Time Needed: 20 to 45 minutes, depending on the time limits set by players.

Supplies: Pencil and paper for each player, and a timekeeper.

What's It All About?

To "scoop" as much "troop" as you can in a given amount of time. "Scooping" is getting points for finding police cars, law enforcement officers, etc., in certain situations or under certain conditions.

How to Start Scooping

1. All players familiarize themselves with the Trooper Scooper Lists below and their corresponding point values.
2. Next, players set a time limit for the game.
3. Beginning together, players go scooping, point out their findings, and record their points on paper. All findings must be confirmed by at least one other player or someone not in the game.

And the Winner Is...

The player who scoops the most troop in the course of the game.

CAUTION

If your car is pulled over during the game, the trooper wins, all players are scooped, and the game is over.

1 Point:

local police car from town you are driving
  in
cop walking a beat
police station
cop directing traffic
police car stopped with one cop inside

2 Points:

police sign
police phone
out-of-state cop car with 2 cops inside
cop outside stopped car
trooper headquarters (State Police)
cop car with lights flashing
2 cop cars stopped side by side

4 Points:

police truck
paddy wagon
cop on a horse
cop car with lights and siren on
cop car with female cop driving

cop looking at license by stopped car
cop talking on radio inside car
cop car passing your car while moving
motorcycle cop
cop eating
cop car stopped at restaurant or gas
  station

7 Points:

cop car in accident
hidden cop car (behind trees, side roads,
  etc.)
cop car with male and female officers
  inside
your car passes cop car
motorcycle cop with lights and siren on

9 Points:

cop car with defects: flat tire, hood up,
  in tow, broken taillight, etc.
cop sleeping inside car
cop waving back at you

Beth's Facts in Five

Here's a fun game where players test their skills in *car*tegories that they select.

How Many Can Play? Any number.

Best Playing Conditions: Whenever and wherever you want to, regardless of traffic conditions.

Time Needed: 5 to 15 minutes.

Supplies: Pencil and paper for each player, and a timekeeper.

How to Play

1. Each player draws a rectangular box with five columns across and five rows down, as shown in the illustration.

	TREES	SONGS	CARS	CITIES	FOOD
E			Eldorado		
L			Lincoln		
G			Geo		
P			Porsche		
H			Honda		

2. Then, going in turns, each player picks one *car*tegory to write above each column until all five are labeled. Suggested *car*tegories are: Trees, Food, Cars, Movies, Songs, Cities, Countries, and Names.

3. Next, players take turns picking one letter to head each of the five rows. They write them at the left side of the rectangle (see illustration).

4. When all players are ready, everyone has 5 minutes to fill in as many boxes as they can with names of things in each *car*tegory that start with the letter heading each row. Example: in the Cars column, Beth wrote Eldorado, Lincoln, Geo, Porsche, and Honda.

5. When time is up, all players share their answers. If any players have the same answer they have to cross them off their papers. One point is given for each correct answer.

And the Winner Is . . .

The player with the most points.

The *Road*io Roundup

Here's a number roundup game where players search for numbers outside the car that come up on the display window of their car radio.

How Many Can Play? Any number.
Best Playing Conditions: It's more fun at night, but daytime is okay; highway traveling with medium to heavy traffic is best.
Time Needed: 30 to 45 minutes.
Supplies: Pencil and paper for each player, a timekeeper, and a car radio with a scanning or seeking mode and (LED) display window.

Starting the *Road*io Roundup

1. One player sitting in the front is appointed the DJ for the game.
2. The DJ watches the station numbers in the display window as she presses the scan or seek button on the radio.

NOTE: On most car radios the scan mode will automatically move from one preset station to the next and the seek mode will seek and find the strongest signals in the area your car is passing through.

3. Players now decide which mode they will use in the game and how many rounds they will play.

How to Play

1. The DJ tells each player, going in order one at a time, the channel that comes up in the window. The player then begins a 3-minute search outside the car for the numbers that make up the channel showing.
2. Players can use numbers from any source outside the car (license plates, road signs, building numbers, etc.).
3. Points are won and recorded as shown in the following example.

Roundup Chart

Example: Elise is the DJ and also the first player. She presses the seek button and the dial stops at 92.3.

She will get: 1 point for each number 9, 2, or 3 she sees; 2 points for each 14, the *sum* of her numbers 9 + 2 + 3; 3 points for finding any two of her numbers in a row—92 or 23; and 4 points for finding *all* of her numbers in a row—923.

And the Winner Is...

The *road*io player with the most points after all rounds are played.

The Crowded Toll Plaza

Here's one good way for everyone to survive the misery of crawling through a crowded toll plaza.

How Many Can Play? Any number.
Best Playing Conditions: Crowded toll plazas.
Time Needed: Let's hope no longer than 10 minutes.
Supplies: Pencil and paper for each player.

What's It All About?

To get as many points as you can from seeing targets around your car before it passes through the tollbooth.

How to Play

1. The game begins when your car comes to its first complete stop at a crowded toll station.
2. Going all at once, players try to find as many of the targets listed below as they can and keep a running total of their points.
3. Each target is worth 1 point, can only be used once, and must be identified and announced as it is seen. Example: "Vanity plate on the green Cadillac over there."
4. During the game, any player has the option to select one vehicle behind their car that he thinks will get through the tollgate before his own. Each player whose prediction comes true is awarded 5 bonus points. For each prediction that does not come true, 3 points are deducted.
5. As your car approaches the tollbooth, the player with the most points must make any toll plaza worker or any other driver wave or say "Hi" or "Hello," or forfeit the game to the player nearest in points to him.
6. In the case of a tie, all players with the same score must complete #5. The first one to succeed will be the winner.

And the Winner Is...

The player who scores the most points and makes it through event #5 first. (And don't forget to figure in those bonus points for the players who take the option.)

TARGETS LIST

Cars with:

- a vanity plate
- an out-of-state plate
- a dog in it
- no front plate
- bumper stickers
- no bumper stickers
- mag wheels
- wire wheels
- a luggage rack
- a piece of furniture on top
- the convertible top down
- a hood ornament
- a passenger in the back seat only
- a panting dog inside
- anyone sitting backwards
- only a driver in it
- whitewall tires
- a directional on
- no hubcap on one wheel
- three children inside
- the convertible top up
- a college decal in the window
- a Turbo sign
- a dog's head sticking out the window

 Don't forget, you can make up your own targets too.

The *Beeping* Tom Game

How Many Can Play? Two.
Best Playing Conditions: City
or highway travel when
traffic is medium to heavy;
toll plazas can be helpful.
Time Needed: 10 to 30
minutes, depending on the
length of your lists.
Supplies: Pencil and paper for
each player.

What's It All About?

You and your opponent will be looking *inside* the cars around you to find objects or to see things that people are doing or wearing, etc.

How to Play

1. First, each player makes a list of five to ten things for his opponent to find. The number of things you choose is up to you, depending on how long you want the game to last. If you need help there's a big list of suggested "things," opposite.
2. Next, players exchange lists and read them carefully to make sure they understand what to look for.
3. When both players are ready, they begin their search by looking for any item on their lists. They do not have to find them in order.
4. When items are found they must be called out and confirmed by the other player.

And the Winner Is...

The first player to find all items on his list, or an agreed-upon total, and then make someone outside the car wave at him.

SUGGESTED THINGS LIST

- someone reading
- a woman wearing a hat
- a dog or cat
- car with object hanging from rearview mirror
- car with driver's window down
- woman with glasses on
- passenger with seatbelt on
- driver with hat on
- car with 3 people in front seat
- someone sitting backwards
- child sleeping
- car with 2 passengers in back seat only
- person wearing headphones
- car with no passengers
- anyone sleeping
- a driver smoking
- man in white shirt
- person with sunglasses on
- car with all people inside wearing glasses
- male driver with T-shirt on
- a baby seat
- person wearing baseball cap
- car with 1 woman and 1 child inside

What's on Your Plate?

This game is played using the numbers and letters you find on license plates of the cars, trucks, buses, etc., around you.

How Many Can Play? Any number.

Best Playing Conditions: On the highway or in town when traffic is medium to heavy.

Time Needed: 20 to 45 minutes.

Supplies: Pencil and paper for each player.

What's It All About?

Each player must find the ten Things on the Plate in the order that they are listed.

To Get Started

1. All players read through the ten things they will be looking for.
2. Next, all players write the numbers 1 through 10 on their paper.
3. Then, next to each number, players write the letter(s) or number(s) they will be looking for when the game starts.

How to Play

1. All players start looking at the same time for their things. (Remember: You must start with number 1, then 2, 3, etc.)
2. When players find an item, they point it out to at least one other player, cross out the number corresponding to that item, and go on to the next one.

And the Winner Is...

The first player to find all ten Things on the Plate.

THINGS ON THE PLATE

1. Your own initials; only your first and last, and they do not have to be found in order.
2. The number of people in your car. (Don't forget yourself!)
3. The first letter of the current month (April . . . May . . . June . . . etc.).
4. The last letter in the make of your car (Nissan, Buick, Toyota, Honda, etc.).
5. The second letter of your driver's first name (Cecil, Pat, Arne, etc.).
6. The number of people in the back seat of your car.
7. What 2 minus 2 equals.
8. What 2 multiplied by 4 equals.
9. A 2-letter word.
10. A 3-letter word. The letters do not have to be in order.

Remember to look for Jumblewords or Scramblewords. (Example: In the letters OTE you can make the words TO and TOE. In TBU there is BUT and TUB.)

Your New Car Game

The fast and easy way to get that new car, with no money down, no monthly payments, and no hidden charges!

How Many Can Play? Anyone who would like a new car.
Best Playing Conditions: When the old jalopy breaks down on the way to vacationland.
Time Needed: 5 minutes.
Supplies: Just a lucky number!

How to Play

1. Pick a number between 1 and 30 (or 40, or 50, etc.), and announce it to the other car shoppers.
2. Going one at a time or all at once, count the cars passing in the opposite direction until your *new car* arrives!

And the Winner Is . . .

Everyone's a winner, of a "new" car, in this game—but will it be your dream machine or a nightmare?!

Zingers

Here's a great way to transform hours of monotonous highway travel into hilarious fun. Works great at night, too!

> **How Many Can Play?** Two.
> **Best Playing Conditions:** Long highway trips, day or night, when visibility is good and traffic is steady.
> **Time Needed:** 1 to 3 hours.
> **Supplies:** Cool heads and eyes like a hawk.

What's It All About?

You and your opponent will be looking for numbers or letters, in order, only on license plates passing by your car.

How to Play

1. First, you and your opponent decide what each of you will be hunting for: One of you will be looking for the letters A through I in order. The other will look for the numbers 1 through 9 in order.
2. When you are both ready, each of you starts looking at the same time, and calls out the letters and numbers as you find them. (It is best to use plates from cars traveling in your direction for this game.)

How to Get into Double Trouble

1. As soon as the letter hunter finds an F and the number hunter finds a 6, both players can start looking for any double letter (AA, FF, MM, etc.) or double number (22, 77, 33, etc.) combination. These are called *zingers*, and can be used by either player to make an opponent go back and find *again* the letter or number she had just found.
2. Players cannot be bumped back below F or 6.
3. Of course, while this is going on, players continue to search for their single letters or numbers until one of them gets to the end of her search.

And the Winner Is...

The letter hunter who reaches I or the number hunter who reaches 9 *before* the other.

Since letters are a bit harder to find than numbers, players who go in rounds should alternate categories.

The Raindrop Race

Here's a little game for diehard racers to play during a light rainfall, or after the rain stops.

How Many Can Play? Two is best, but more can play if there's room.

Best Playing Conditions: When light rain is falling, or just after the rain stops.

Time Needed: 5 minutes.

Supplies: The side windows of your car.

How to Play

1. Each player positions herself on the back seat so that she can see the "tracks" of the raindrops up close.
2. Next, all racers pick a raindrop near the top of the windowpane.
3. When all racers are on their mark, one of them says "Go," and each player tracks the course of her drop toward the bottom.

And the Winner Is...

The player whose drop reaches the bottom first, or, if you want to play with a time limit, the one who gets closest to the bottom when the time is up.

Any drop that joins forces with other drops or streams still belongs to its original owner. Remember to leave enough space between racers so your drops don't come together.

Seeing in the Rain

Who says you can't have fun when it's raining???

How Many Can Play? Any number.

Best Playing Conditions: City or highway travel when it looks like it's going to rain.

Time Needed: 15 to 30 minutes.

Supplies: Pencil and paper for each player, and a good set of windshield wipers.

What's It All About?

When it looks like it's going to rain, players are invited to join this game. They will be getting points for things they will be seeing outside the car as a result of the "bad" weather.

How to Play

1. All players familiarize themselves with the items on the Target List, and set a time limit for the game.
2. The player who sees (and shows proof of) the first raindrop to hit the car gets 1 point and starts the game.
3. Beginning together, players hunt for the items, call them out to at least one other player, and keep track of their scores.
4. One point is given for each citing, and items can be used only once by the player who sees them *first*. Other players can find the same target but must spot it in a different place.

And the Winner Is...

The player who accumulates the most points by the end of the game.

And the Anytime, Automatic Winner Is...

The player who first sees a rainbow or a mirage on the road.

TARGET LIST

Can you be the *first* one to see a (an):

- bolt of lightning
- car with wipers on
- car with headlights on (while it is still light)
- person holding something overhead for protection
- car with wipers *off* during rain
- window of car all the way down during steady rainfall
- car stopped on roadside due to downpour
- convertible putting top up in the rain
- driver wiping inside of windshield with hand
- car with rear wiper going
- car with emergency flashers going
- car with directional signal left on too long
- Slippery When Wet sign
- car with only one headlight on in the rain
- convertible with top down
- person running to get out of the rain
- driver or passenger with hand out the window to see if it's raining
- driver or passenger rolling up a window
- pedestrian looking up to the sky
- pedestrian holding hand out to tell if it's raining
- person opening an umbrella
- person with umbrella turned inside out
- umbrella in a trash can
- umbrella being used by more than one person

WORD GAMES

Sign Language

What? You didn't know that signs could speak to you?

How Many Can Play? Any number.
Best Playing Conditions: Highway or city travel where road signs are seen.
Time Needed: 15 to 30 minutes.
Supplies: Pencil and paper for each player, and players who love to play with words.

What's It All About?

In this game, players will be competing against time and each other to form complete sentences out of the letters found on road signs.

How to Play

1. First, all players agree on a word (for example, *Mobil*), or a series of words (for example, *Dead End*) taken from road signs.
2. After the word(s) has been chosen and all players are ready, someone says "Go."
3. Each player now tries to form a complete sentence out of the word using each consecutive letter of the word as the first letter of a new word in the sentence.
4. The first player to form her sentence calls out "Stop," and reads it to the other players. Each word in the sentence earns 1 point. Example: Angela and Wendy decide to use the word *Mobil* and begin the game. After a minute, Angela calls "Stop" and reads her sentence to Wendy: "Move over, Becky, I'm leaving." At 1 point per word, Angela is now in the lead 5 to 0. Next they choose a Dead End sign to work with. This time Wendy calls "Stop" and reads her sentence to Angela: "Detective Earl arrested Doctor Eastlake's notorious daughter." Now Wendy is ahead 7 to 5.
5. Play continues in this manner until one player reaches a game point total (25, 50, etc.).

And the Winner Is...

The SIGN LANGUAGE player who gets to the game point total first.

Rider's Cramp

A good soap opera substitute for tall tales and budding, unpublished novelists.

How to Get Rid of Rider's Cramp

1. To break the *rider's* block, one player begins a story by saying only the first three (or four, or five . . .) words of it.
2. Going one at a time and in turn, all other players follow in order and add three (or four, or five . . .) words of their own until the story comes to an agreeable ending.

And the Winner Is . . .

Determined by a vote: to determine which *Road's* Scholar deserves the *Mobel* Prize for Litera*tour*.

The Alphabet Games (I, II, and III)

Here are *three* easy-to-play alphabet games to help you get to the next Rest Area.

How Many Can Play? Any number.

Best Playing Conditions: City or highway travel with plenty of things to see.

Time Needed: 20 to 45 minutes.

Supplies: Pencil, paper, and a "memory bank" with 26 safety deposit boxes inside.

Game I

How to Play

1. Going one at a time, in turns, each player must choose a word for each letter of the alphabet. (If there are three players, there will be three different words beginning with A, B, C, etc.)
2. As the game continues, each player must repeat all of the previous words before adding a new one that begins with the next letter.

And the Winner Is...

Determined by elimination.

Game II

How to Play

1. Beginning at the same time, and *without* using license plates or letters from road signs, each player must find an object outside the car for each consecutive letter of the alphabet. Example: airplane, Buick, car, driver, evergreen, Fotomat, etc.
2. If necessary, for the letters K, Q, X, Y, and Z players may use license plates.

And the Winner Is...

The player who reaches the end of the alphabet first.

Game III

How to Play

1. Beginning at the same time, and using *only* letters from license plates on cars passing their own, players must make up a word of at least four letters in length for each consecutive letter of the alphabet. Examples: PQ7 99A—"apple, over there," or 884 PBX—"boat on that Mercedes," C19 444—"candy."
2. One point is awarded for each correct word, and players do not have to announce when they find a target letter, only when they have thought of a word to make from it.
3. Players keep records of their individual scores.

And the Winner Is...

The first player who, reaching the end of the alphabet, calls out a word beginning with Z that is at least four letters long.

The Out-of-State Plate Game

Here's a four-stage, boredom-beating game that's guaranteed to gobble up at least 30 minutes worth of Exit signs (that aren't yours!).

How Many Can Play? Any number.
Best Playing Conditions: Interstate highway travel with medium to heavy traffic.
Time Needed: 30 to 45 minutes.
Supplies: Pencil and paper.

How to Play

Stage I: Beginning at the same time, each player must start the game by finding his own out-of-state license plate and calling out the name of the state it comes from. For this game, an out-of-state plate is one from a *different* state than the one in which your car is registered and the one in which you are driving during the game.

Stage II: Next, each player must find and call out all the letters of the alphabet in correct order as they are observed on any license plate. During this stage of the game, each player can make up to five substitutions by using any double letter (AA, KK, LL, etc.) combination she sees on license plates in place of one letter she cannot find.

Stage III: Then, using any three letters found on one plate, each player must make up one word (of at least four letters) for each of the letters found. All words must *begin* with the found letters. Example: WGN 447 could be <u>We</u>'re <u>g</u>oing <u>n</u>owhere.

Stage IV: Finally, after completing the first three stages, all players must find another out-of-state plate and call out which state it comes from.

And the Winner Is...

The player who first completes all four stages.

The Country-City Game

Here's a good way to pass some time and brush up on your geography while you're doing it.

What's It All About?

This game is played like THE CARNATION GAME, except in this one players connect country names with the names of cities around the world.

How to Play

1. Player #1 starts the game by naming a country.
2. Within 30 seconds, player #2 must name a city whose first letter is the same as the last letter of the previously named country. Example: Ethiopia... Albuquerque... England... Denver... Russia, etc.
3. Play continues in this manner with players going in turns.

And the Winner Is...

Determined by elimination.

The Measured Mile Games (I and II)

Put those measured mile markers to good use with these two games.

How Many Can Play? Any number.
Best Playing Conditions: Highway travel where measured mile markers are posted.
Time Needed: 5 to 10 minutes.
Supplies: Pencil and paper for each player, and a "starter" to watch for the mile markers.

Game I

How to Get Started

1. Ask your driver to watch out for the signs announcing the measured mile area ahead.
2. All players get ready to look for words, objects, car makes and models, etc., that start with the letters that spell Measured Mile.
3. Words and objects can be found for each letter as they appear in sequence, one object per letter (M, E, A, etc.), or in random order with players trying to get as many things as possible. Players decide which way they will play. The words corresponding to the letters can be written down or called out by each player.

How to Play

1. Have your driver or someone not playing start the game by saying "Go" when your car passes the first marker.
2. Players now make note of things they spot as their car passes through the measured mile.
3. When your car passes the second marker, starter ends the game by saying "Stop."

And the Winner Is...

The player with the most words or objects at the end of the game.

Players can make up their own variations of the game using food items, cities, famous personalities, countries, etc.

Game II

Is It a Mile Yet?

In this second MEASURED MILE GAME, when your driver announces the beginning of the measured mile, all players close their eyes and keep them closed until they think the car has passed the second marker.

And the Winner Is...

The player who calls, "Mile's up" when your car is closest to the second marker.

The 18-Wheeler Dealer

Or...how far into the future can you see?

How Many Can Play? Any number.

Best Playing Conditions: Interstate highway travel where you're likely to see lots of tractor-trailer trucks.

Time Needed: 45 to 90 minutes.

Supplies: Pencil and paper for each player.

What's It All About?

You and your opponents will be winning points for predictions that come true on the inside and outside of tractor-trailers!

How to Play

1. Players keep their eyes out for tractor-trailers in the distance that are traveling in the same direction as their car.

NOTE: In order to use a truck for the game, players must be reasonably sure that their car will overtake it eventually. (Don't worry...you'll catch it on the next hill.)

2. Going one at a time, each player uses the chart, opposite, (or writes down on a separate piece of paper) and fills in his predictions of what will (or will not) be seen when the truck is within sight. One point is given for each correct prediction, including predictions of zero if they come true.

3. Points are totaled when the truck has passed your car or your car has passed it.

And the Winner Is...

The wheeler-dealer who scores the most points at the end of all the rounds.

Remember, if another truck doesn't show up right away, game results can be set aside until one does.

THE DEALER CHART

1. Number of state decals on the side of the truck. _____
2. Colors of state decals on the side of the truck (pick three). _____
3. Number of license plates on the rear end of the truck. _____
4. Number of moving tires. _____
5. Number of spare tires. _____
6. Colors of license plates on front and rear of truck (pick three). _____
7. Make of the truck (Mack, White, Kenworth, Peterbuilt, Autocar, etc.) _____
8. Number of people in the cab. _____
9. Number of men in the cab. _____
10. Number of women in the cab. _____
11. Number of children in the cab. _____
12. Whether there are any dogs or other pets in the cab. (yes or no) _____
13. Whether the driver is wearing a hat. (yes or no) _____
14. Whether the driver has a tattoo. (yes or no) _____
15. Whether the driver is wearing glasses, other than sunglasses. (yes or no) _____
16. Whether the driver is wearing sunglasses. (yes or no) _____

BONUS POINTS

2 points: Make the driver wave
3 points: Make the driver give the OK sign
4 points: Make the driver give the peace sign
5 points: Make the driver blow his horn

The *Car*voyant Game

Here's a little game that tests telepathic skills of the players as they predict objects that will be seen in an area their car hasn't come to yet.

How to Play

1. First, all players decide on a target area they will be using for their predictions. Example: the far side of a big hill, a town or place you will be in soon, beyond a distant landmark, etc.
2. Next, players now decide how many predictions they will make, and each one writes his own predictions on paper. Example: a church steeple, a Stop sign, a US Mail truck, a black dog, a gas station sign, a motorcycle, a Honda, etc.
3. When the target area comes into view, each player hunts for his predictions for a 5-minute search period.
4. As predictions are seen, players must call them out, and 1 point is awarded for each correct prediction. Play can continue in rounds.

And the Winner Is...

The *car*voyant with the most points after all rounds have been played.

A shorter version of THE CAR-VOYANT GAME can also be played by closing your eyes, predicting the things you will see, then opening them to see how many are there.

Make Someone ???? Game

Did you ever get the urge to make that passenger in the car next to yours look over at you?

How Many Can Play? Any number.
Best Playing Conditions: Town or city travel when traffic is moving slowly; traffic jams are perfect.
Time Needed: 15 to 30 minutes.
Supplies: Pencil and paper.

What's It All About?

Players in this game will be winning points for getting people outside the car to make expressions, gestures, or signs in response to ones that they make.

How to Play

1. Going one at a time and in turns, player #1 chooses a response and assigns it to player #2. Suggested responses: smile, yawn, laugh, scratch head, wave, peace sign, point finger, OK sign, funny face, sad face, etc.
2. When player #2 is ready, he says "Go" and has 60 seconds to make someone outside the car do what player #1 has called for.
3. One point is awarded for each successful response, and players can try for as many responses as they wish in their 60-second time period.
4. Players continue until a game point total is reached, or an agreed-upon time period is up.

And the Winner Is...

The player who reaches the game point total first, or the one with the most points when the time period is up.

Players can vary the game by choosing their own responses to find ("I can make someone look over at us."), changing time limits, and making up new responses.

The Baggage Claim Game

Getting out of the baggage claim area is one of the most satisfying experiences of your trip. Here's a way to prepare for it.

How Many Can Play? Any number, but two works the best.
Best Playing Conditions: After you get tired of doing nothing.
Time Needed: 20 to 40 minutes.
Supplies: Pencil and paper for each player, and a little X-ray vision wouldn't hurt.

Getting Packed

1. Each player writes a list of ten items that describes her make-believe baggage, being sure that no one sees what she's writing. Item One is the color of her suitcases (only one color) and Item Two is the number of pieces in the set. (See the Sample Baggage List, opposite.) Sets are limited to ten pieces.
2. Next, players write down seven items of clothing or travel gear that are packed in their imaginary suitcases. These are Items Three through Nine.
3. Finally, each player enters in Item Ten a number between 1 and 20. This is her baggage claim number.

How to Play

1. Player #1 has three chances to guess the color (Item One) on her opponent's list. If she does not guess correctly in her three chances, she must try again in her next turn until she does. If she guesses correctly, she goes on to guess the number of pieces (Item Two). Items One and Two must be guessed, in order, before players can proceed in the same way through the remaining list.
2. For Items Three through Nine, players give the first letter of the item to their opponent as a clue.

And the Winner Is . . .

The first player to get her baggage claim number and get out of the area.

SAMPLE BAGGAGE LIST

Item	1.	Color of suitcase	Red
Item	2.	Number of pieces	6
Item	3.	Deodorant	(D)
Item	4.	Razor	(R)
Item	5.	T-Shirt	(T)
Item	6.	Bathing suit	(B)
Item	7.	Camera	(C)
Item	8.	Towel	(T)
Item	9.	Sneakers	(S)
Item	10.	Baggage claim number	10

Bored on Board

Here's a simple game for word lovers to play after all the crosswords and acrostics are done...or almost done.

Players may award bonus points for words formed in special categories (proper names, films, book titles, authors, countries, etc.).

74

How to Play

1. Each player draws the BORED ON BOARD grid (as shown below) on his paper.
2. When all players are ready, each one begins to fill in the squares of the grid.
3. Moving from left to right on the grid, the first column must have a three-letter word, the second column a four-letter word, the third column a five-letter word, the fourth column a six-letter word, and the fifth column a seven-letter word.
4. All words formed must contain the vertical and horizontal letters that correspond to the square they are in. The letters can be used in any order. (See example below.)

And the Winner Is...

The first player to complete the grid.

	B	O	A	R	D
B	BIB	BOWL	BASIC	ROBBIN	BANDITS
O					
R					
E					
D					

Write Up Your Altitude

Here's a fun way to get up to cruising speed, maybe even before the pilot does.

How Many Can Play? Any number.
Best Playing Conditions: On your way up.
Time Needed: 20 to 30 minutes.
Supplies: Pencil and paper for each flyer.

How to Get Up There

Starting on the Runway at the bottom of the Altitude Chart (below), each flyer must rise up through the altitudes in the order that they appear.

And the Winner Is...

The first flyer to reach 30,000 feet with his paper airplane.

ALTITUDE CHART

END
30,000 feet: Write the number 30,000 out in letters (t-h-i-r-t-y t-h-o-u-s-a-n-d) on your paper, pick 3 of the letters and write down 3 different airline companies beginning with the letters you've picked.

20,000 feet: Write down a three-, a four-, and a five-letter word that all begin with the letter of the row you are sitting in.

10,000 feet: Take your city of destination and write down the name of an animal for each letter of the city. (Example: Chicago—cat, horse, impala, cougar, etc.)

5,000 feet: Find the first name of one of your flight attendants and write down the name of a foreign city, a foreign country, or a planet for each letter of his or her name.

1,000 feet: Write down a food item for each letter of the name of the airline you are traveling on.

Runway: Write down an American city for each letter of your first name. (Example: Danny—Denver, Atlanta, New York, Nashville, Youngstown.)

START

A Star Is *Airborne*

You and your opponent are going to get five of your favorite "stars" to join you in the air. That is, *if* you can remember the name of the airline they're coming on.

How Many Can Play? Two.
Best Playing Conditions:
When you're closest to the "stars" and you'd like them on board.
Time Needed: 10 to 20 minutes.
Supplies: Pencil and paper for two, and a few empty seats nearby. A timekeeper too.

To Get Ready

Each player writes the names of five of their favorite stars (rock groups, movie stars, dancers, etc.) on paper. Lists should be kept secret.

How to Get Them on Board

1. When both players are ready, Arlene gives Claude a flight number between 1 and 20. Let's say it is 8.
2. Claude now counts eight letters into his star list and draws a line underneath the eighth letter. (See the example above right.) He now has 15 seconds to name an airline that begins with this eighth letter. If he can name one (like Avianca), he writes its name in the margin and his first star is on board.
3. If Claude cannot think of an airline, he tells Arlene his letter and

Arlene	Claude
Charlie Sheen	Miki Howard
The Smiths	Soul II Soul
Denzel	Donald Sutherland
Washington	K. D. Laing
The Red Hot Chili	Kevin Costner
Peppers	
Heavy D & The	
Boyz	

she now has 15 seconds to think of one that begins with this letter. If she succeeds, she writes the airline next to any one of her stars.

4. Play continues now with Claude calling a flight number for Arlene.

Runway Rules

1. A player who correctly names an airline for her star gets to go again until she misses.
2. If a flight number lands on a star who is already on board, the

player repeats the flight number until she lands on one that is not.

3. Airlines cannot be used more than once.

4. For airlines that begin with *Air* or *Aero*, it is okay to use the first letter of the second word in its name. (Examples: In Air <u>F</u>rance, the <u>F</u> is okay; in Aero <u>M</u>exico, the <u>M</u> is okay.)

And the Winner Is...

The first player to get all of her "stars" *air*borne.

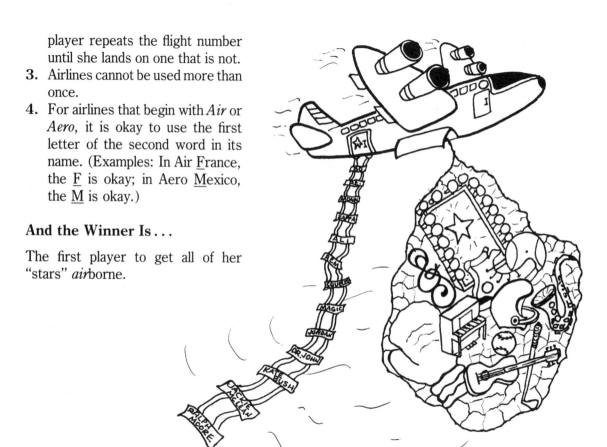

Wingo

For Bingo buffs, an airline version with a categorical twist.

How Many Can Play? Any number.

Best Playing Conditions: When the airborne Bingo urge overwhelms you.

Time Needed: 15 to 25 minutes.

Supplies: Pencil and paper for each player.

How to Play

1. Players should draw their own playing squares to form a playing card (opposite).
2. Next, players think of the names of five airlines to write along the left side of the square, and five categories they want to use across the top of the square. All players should use the same airlines and the same categories.
3. Using only the letters of the airlines beside their boxes, players must think of three words for each category in every column.
4. Boxes must have three words in them before WINGO lines can be drawn.
5. Players enter words as they think of them, and try to spell WINGO by getting three words per box and then drawing their WINGO lines for a victory.

And the Winner Is...

The first player to complete the squares, using the diagonal boxes, the horizontal boxes, or the vertical boxes. But players must have three words per box before that box is considered complete.

WINGO

	W	I	N	G	O
	FOOD	FOREIGN CITIES	CARS	FIRST NAMES	COUNTRIES
EASTERN	Eggs Sausage Toast				
PAN AM		Paris Madrid Naples			
VARIG			Volvo Alfa-Romeo Geo		
AIR INDIA				Alex Raul Inez	
DELTA					Denmark England Turkey

Getting Off the Ground

Sometimes, getting to the airport *and* getting into the air just doesn't work out the way you thought it would! Here's a little game that should provide an illustration.

How Many Can Play? Two is best, but more can play also.
Best Playing Conditions: When you can stand to be frustrated.
Time Needed: 30 to 45 minutes.
Supplies: Pencil and paper for each player, and a few good strokes of luck.

What's It All About?

1. Each player will be advancing through the 10 Steps to Take-off, moving one step at a time. As each step is reached, the player writes his or her initials on the line beside it.
2. Next, each player writes the numbers 1 through 20 on paper in any order she wishes. (Example: 6, 2, 4, 17, 20, 14, 9, 12 ... etc.) Count them to make sure you've got all 20 numbers.

---

10 STEPS TO TAKE-OFF

1. Pack your bags ⸺⸺⸺
2. Ride to the airport ⸺⸺⸺
3. Find parking ⸺⸺⸺
4. Check in ⸺⸺⸺
5. Go through security ⸺⸺⸺
6. Boarding A through M ⸺⸺⸺
7. Boarding N through Z ⸺⸺⸺
8. Taxi to runway ⸺⸺⸺
9. Line up to take off ⸺⸺⸺
10. Take off ⸺⸺⸺

How to Play

1. Each player pencils in her initials next to "pack your bags" and player #1 calls out the first number on her 1 to 20 list. Let's say the number is 12. Players should cross off numbers as they are called to remember where they left off.
2. Player #2 now finds #12 on the Ups & Downs List (right). Following the instructions next to that number, she now makes her corresponding move into the 10 Steps to Take-off.
3. The game continues in this way, with players going back and forth using each other's numbers to move ahead *or* go back on the 10 Steps to Take-off list until one of them takes off.

Ups and Downs List

1. Car won't start — Go back one space.
2. Flat tire — Stay where you are.
3. Sleep at friend's house near airport — Go ahead two spaces.
4. Forgot your luggage — Go back home to pack your bags.
5. Shortcut to airport saves half an hour — Go ahead two spaces.
6. No lines at check-in — Go ahead one space.
7. Can't find your keys — Go back one space.
8. Limo service — Go ahead one space.
9. Seat sold twice — Go back one space.
10. Leave two hours early — Go ahead one space.
11. Flight cancelled — Go back one space
12. Ride behind ambulance — Go ahead one space.
13. Sudden storm delay — Stay where you are and miss next turn.
14. Pulled over for "running" a stop sign — Stay where you are.
15. Take train to plane — Go ahead one space.
16. Heavy traffic — Go back one space.
17. Rich friend flies you to airport in helicopter — Go ahead two spaces.
18. Lost tickets — Go back one space.
19. No traffic — Go ahead one space.
20. Ride with diplomat — Go ahead two spaces.

Runway Rules

Players must land *exactly* on Take-off to win, and cannot be pushed back from #1, "Pack your bags."

And the Winner Is...

The first player to land directly on Take-off.

20 Conjetures

Conjecture: to guess or infer from inconclusive evidence.
Conjeture: to guess or infer from inconclusive evidence on a jet.

How Many Can Play? Any number.
Best Playing Conditions: When time isn't flying and tic-tac-toe won't cut it.
Time Needed: 20 to 40 minutes.
Supplies: Pencil, paper, and a fancy for the plane things.

How to Play

1. Player #1 thinks of an object inside the airplane . . . like the little cut on the flight attendant's chin where he nicked himself shaving!
2. Other players are allowed 20 conjetures (in total, not 20 each) to guess what the object is.
3. Guesses must be answerable by yes or no responses.
4. If the players have not guessed the object after the 20 conjetures, player #1 is the winner of the round. After player #1 reveals the answer, the game continues with player #2 picking a new object for the other players to look for.

First try to determine which area of the plane the object is in. (More than three rows ahead of yours? Left or right of the aisle? Is it moving?) Don't waste your conjetures by guessing wildly.

And the Winner Is . . .

The player who has won the most rounds.

Reaching for the Stars

Okay "star" lovers, here's your chance to shine.

How Many Can Play? Any number.
Best Playing Conditions: When you feel really close to the stars.
Time Needed: 15 to 30 minutes.
Supplies: Pencil and paper for each player, and enough personality(s) for your *initial* success.

Where to Find Them

Just like the FAMOUS CARACTERS game, you'll be looking for them in the column of initials you'll be making up, only this time they're going to appear out of airline companies. So get those rock groups, rap crews, and basketball stars ready!

How to Play

1. Each player writes the alphabet in a vertical column as shown on page 39, in the game FAMOUS CARACTERS.
2. Next, one player thinks of airline companies and writes in their names vertically next to the letters of the alphabet, creating a list of two initials. All players use the same list of letters. It's okay if you have more letters than you need as long as there is a letter next to Z.
3. After players decide how long the game will last, each one tries to think of as many "stars" as they can from the initials in the column. See page 39.
4. One point is given for each correct star.

And the Winner Is...

The player with the most star points when the time limit is up.

If you aren't reaching enough stars or you want to play longer, just start with a new group of airlines.

83

Terminal Boredom

Stop terminal boredom now! And with this game you have everything you need to do it!

How Many Can Play? Any number.

Best Playing Conditions: When you're stuck in a terminal and monotony is turning into boredom.

Time Needed: 20 to 40 minutes.

Supplies: Pencil, paper, and the powers of observation.

What's It All About?

1. In an agreed-upon time period, all players must find as many items as they can from the Terminal Playing Ground. They can look for the items in any order they wish.
2. Points are awarded according to the point values as listed below.

Starting Out on the Search

1. First, all players look over the items in the Terminal Playing Ground and take note of their point values.
2. Next, players decide how long their search periods will last and if they want to play more than one round.
3. When all players are ready, the search begins for the items. When items are found, players must call them out for their opponent(s) to see and then write down the number of that item. Items can only be used once by the player who finds them first. Other players must look for their own examples of them in the Terminal Playing Ground.

And the Winner Is . . .

The player who has accumulated the most points at the end of the search.

Remember, players can make up another Playing Ground list when these items get boring.

Terminal Playing Ground

5 Points

1. an exit sign
2. man carrying a suitbag
3. men's room sign
4. person carrying no bags
5. man with attache case
6. a cigarette ad
7. a fire extinguisher
8. person reading a newspaper or magazine
9. person reading a book
10. woman in high heels
11. man with glasses on
12. women's room sign

7 Points

13. woman in sneakers
14. person pulling a suitcase
15. airport maintenance worker cleaning
16. woman with only one bag
17. someone smoking a cigarette
18. woman on the telephone
19. A Red Cap or Porter
20. man on the telephone
21. A child without sneakers on
22. an ad for an airline
23. woman with a suitbag
24. man carrying a baby

10 Points

25. man smoking cigar
26. person with animal carrier
27. woman carrying baby
28. person sleeping
29. man with low-top sneakers on
30. woman pushing baby stroller
31. person with three suitcases
32. man with newspaper under his arm
33. woman wearing sunglasses
34. woman wearing boots
35. an ad for an alcoholic beverage
36. a No Smoking sign

The 20-Minute Airline Stew

Here's a fun way to knock off about 500 miles and put your boredom in check.

How Many Can Play? Any number.
Best Playing Conditions: When everyone else is asleep but you and your partner just woke up.
Time Needed: 25 to 40 minutes.
Supplies: Pencil and paper for each player, and a watch to time your stew.

Getting Ready

1. Each player draws the playing grid on her paper (see below).
2. Next, all players decide on 4 airlines to use on the left side of the grid to label the rows.
3. Finally, players choose the four categories they will use and enter them above the columns of the grid. (See sample categories)

How to Start Cooking the Stew

1. Beginning together and moving from left to right, each player has 5 minutes to fill in as many words as possible in the boxes of each vertical column. All words within the categories must begin with a letter found in the name of the airline heading that row.
2. After all four columns have been cooked, players consult the fol-

lowing chart to find out whose stew gets the best score.

How to Judge the Stew

1. All words entered are given 1 point each.
2. Bonus points are awarded as follows:

   In the Scramblewords column, words with four letters get 2 bonus points, words with five letters get 3 bonus points, and words formed with six or more letters get 4 bonus points.

   In the Car Makes or Models column, all foreign cars get 3 bonus points.

   In the Famous People's Initials column, names of musicians get 2 bonus points.

   In the World Cities column, all foreign cities get 2 bonus points.

	SCRAMBLE WORDS	CAR MAKES OR MODELS	FAMOUS PEOPLE'S INITIALS	WORLD CITIES
PAN AM	Man Nap Map Pan Amp	Porsche Audi Maserati Mercedes Alfa Romeo	Paula Abdul Paul McCartney	Paris Madrid Albany New York Portland
DELTA				
UNITED				
U.S. AIR				

3. Players can make up their own bonus point system for the categories they choose.

And the Winner Is...

The airline stew chef who cooks the most points in the 20-minute time limit.

Players should review How to Judge the Stew before playing so that they will know how to maximize their point total. The game will be more exciting if players tally their points after each 5-minute column is completed.

The Jetsetters Game

How many jetsetters can you find hiding in your airline? Maybe enough to win THE JETSETTERS GAME.

How Many Can Play? Any number.

Best Playing Conditions: When you think there may be jetsetters in the airline.

Time Needed: 20 to 40 minutes.

Supplies: Pencil and paper for each player, and a timekeeper.

How to Play

1. First, each player writes down the names of five airline companies under one another on the left side of his paper. Players should all use the same airlines.
2. Next, players decide on a time limit for the game.
3. Then the timekeeper starts the game and each player hunts for the initials of famous people hiding in their airlines.

Example: P A N A M = Paula Abdul, Aaron Neville

D E L T A = Alfonse D'Amato, Duke Ellington

NOTE: In this game, common letters shared by two names (like the A in the Pan Am example) can be used more than once. Also, the last and first letters of an airline can be used for initials but *only* in that order.

4. One point is given for each correct jetsetter.

And the Winner Is ...

The player with the most points when the time limit is up.

Hangarman

Here's a little nick-of-time-killer that everyone will recognize, except when you lose *this* game, instead of getting hung up on a scaffold, you get grounded in the hangar.

How Many Can Play? Two.
Best Playing Conditions:
Right at the point when you're beginning to wish your little brother missed the plane.
Time Needed: 10 to 20 minutes.
Supplies: Pencil and paper.

How to Hang or Get Hung

1. Player #1 thinks of a secret word, counts the number of letters in it, and writes a space for each one on paper.

Example: secret word is
        boredom _ _ _ _ _ _ _

---

2. Player #2 now has to figure out what the word is by guessing letters.
3. If player #2 guesses a letter that is in the word, player #1 writes the letter in its proper space on the line. If the letter guessed is not in the word, player #2 (the one who may get hung) draws the first line of the hangar. (see below).
4. Play continues until player #2 either guesses his opponent's word or winds up in the hangar.

And the Winner Is . . .

The player who gets into the hangar the fewest times.

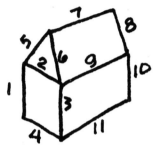

Draw the lines of the hangar in the numbered order.

The "Are We There Yet?" Game

All players predict the exact time (in hours, minutes, and seconds) your car, plane, boat, or train will arrive at it's final destination, or at any place you plan to stop before getting there.

How Many Can Play? Any number.
Best Playing Conditions: Any place, any time, especially when ET whispers the ETA in your ear.
Time Needed: Less than it takes to read this.
Supplies: A timekeeper, pencil and paper for each player, and a view of the future.

How to Play

Each player writes down his arrival time prediction on a sheet of paper, folds it in half, and gives it to the timekeeper.

And the Winner Is...

The player whose estimated time of arrival comes closest to the exact minute when the vehicle you are traveling in comes to a complete and final stop.